Eliza Scudder

Hymns and Sonnets

Eliza Scudder

Hymns and Sonnets

ISBN/EAN: 9783744781497

Printed in Europe, USA, Canada, Australia, Japan

Cover: Foto ©Thomas Meinert / pixelio.de

More available books at **www.hansebooks.com**

Hymns and Sonnets

By E. S.

BOSTON

LOCKWOOD, BROOKS, AND COMPANY

1880

UNIVERSITY PRESS
JOHN WILSON AND SON, CAMBRIDGE

CONTENTS

THE LABURNUM

This young tree's drooping flowers, lovely and fair
And bright as colored by the sun's own glow,
Me-seem, beloved, like the golden hair
That round thy temples gracefully doth flow ;
And, while I at my window sat yestreen,
Through the close-mingling branches of the trees
One only of the blossoms bright was seen
Joyously waving in the summer breeze.
And then I thought how thou hast been to me,
Even as this flower, the only bright fair thing
Which 'mid surrounding shades mine eye could see,
While through dark years I have been journeying
All lonely but for thee.   Heaven help my heart
When the flower withers and thy steps depart !

1845.

TO A YOUNG CHILD

As doth his heart who travels far from home
Leap up whenever he by chance doth see
One from his mother-country lately come,
Friend from my home — thus do I welcome
    thee.
Thou art so late arrived that I the tale
Of thy high lineage on thy brow can trace,
And almost feel the breath of that soft gale
That wafted thee unto this desert place,
And half can hear those ravishing sounds that
    flowed
From out Heaven's gate when it was oped for
    thee,

That thou awhile might'st leave thy bright
    abode
Amid these lone and desolate tracts to be
A homesick, weary wanderer, and then
Return unto thy native land again.

1846.

✠

THE NEW HEAVEN

LET whosoever will, inquire
  Of spirit, or of seer,
To shape unto the heart's desire
  The new life's vision clear.

My God, I rather look to Thee
  Than to these fancies fond,
And wait, till Thou reveal to me
  That fair and far Beyond.

I seek not of Thine Eden-land
  The forms and hues to know, —
What trees in mystic order stand,
  What strange, sweet waters flow ;

What duties fill the heavenly day,
　Or converse glad and kind,
Or how along each shining way
　The bright processions wind.

Oh joy! to hear with sense new born
　The angels' greeting strains,
And sweet to see the first fair morn
　Gild the celestial plains.

But sweeter far to trust in Thee
　While all is yet unknown,
And through the death-dark cheerily
　To walk with Thee alone.

In Thee my powers, my treasures live,
　To Thee my life must tend;
Giving Thyself, Thou all dost give,
　O soul-sufficing friend!

And wherefore should I seek above
Thy city in the sky ?
Since firm in faith and deep in love
Its broad foundations lie ;

Since in a life of peace and prayer,
Nor known on earth, nor praised,
By humblest toil, by ceaseless care,
Its holy towers are raised.

Where pain the soul hath purified,
And penitence hath shriven,
And truth is crowned and glorified,
There — only there — is Heaven.

1855.

THE LOVE OF GOD

Thou Grace Divine, encircling all,
　A soundless, shoreless sea !
Wherein at last our souls must fall,
　O Love of God most free !

When over dizzy heights we go,
　One soft hand blinds our eyes ;
The other leads us safe and slow,　·
　O Love of God most wise !

And though we turn us from Thy face,
　And wander wide and long,
Thou hold'st us still in Thine embrace,
　O Love of God most strong!

The saddened heart, the restless soul, .
    The toil-worn frame and mind,
Alike confess Thy sweet control,
    O Love of God most kind !

But not alone Thy care we claim,
    Our wayward steps to win ;
We know Thee by a dearer name,
    O Love of God within !

And filled and quickened by Thy breath
    Our souls are strong and free
To rise o'er sin and fear and death,
    O Love of God, to Thee !

1852.

EPITAPH ON AN OLD MAID

REST, gentle traveller! on life's toilsome way
Pause here awhile — yet o'er this slumbering
  clay
No weeping, but a joyful tribute pay.

For this green nook, by sun and showers made
  warm,
Gives welcome rest to an o'er-wearied form
Whose mortal life knew many a wintry storm.

Yet, ere the spirit gained a full release
From earth, she had attained that land of
    peace
Where seldom clouds obscure, and tempests
    cease.

No chosen spot of ground she called her
    own ;
In pilgrim guise on earth she wandered on,
Yet alway in her path some flowers were
    strewn.

No dear ones were her own peculiar care,
So was her bounty free as Heaven's air,
For every claim she had enough to spare.

And loving more her heart to give than lend,
Tho' oft deceived in many a trusted friend,
She hoped, believed, and trusted to the end.

She had her joys : ' twas joy to live, to love,
To labor in the world with God above,
And tender hearts that ever near did move.

She had her griefs ; but why recount them
    here, —
The heart-sick loneness, the on-looking fear,
The days of desolation, dark and drear, —

Since every agony left peace behind,
And healing came on every stormy wind,
And still with silver every cloud was lined,

And every loss sublimed some low desire,
And every sorrow taught her to aspire,
Till waiting angels bade her "go up higher."

SUMMER DEPARTING

SHE will not linger ; all in vain thy calling
On the sweet summer ; fair her reign, but brief ;
See'st thou not even now her ripe fruit falling,
And here and there one warning yellow leaf ?
How hath she blessed us ! now let her depart
To gladden other skies, and mourn her not.
Nothing of her, but liveth in the heart ;
Her grace remaineth, though she seems forgot ;
The freshness that hath cheered thy morning
    hours,
The sunset glory that hath lit thine eye,

The night wind's voice, the sweet perfume of
  flowers,
Have passed into thy life, no more to die,
And shall be raised again, in that last day,
When thy first earth and heaven have fled away.

THE DREAMER

I KNOW I dream ; these are no earthly bowers
Wherein the enraptured fancy roams at will.
This warmth, this light, this sunshine and these
    showers
Might ne'er be known to waking sense and skill.
I know I dream — full soon will come the mor-
    row,
With its cold vapors and its leaden sky ;
Yet from these dreamings, hope some hues may
    borrow
To show how fair the lovelier land on high.

I know I dream — but prythee do not wake me,
Let wilful nature have awhile her way ;
Nor will I mourn when these bright hues for-
   sake me,
And melt into the light of common day,
Since to the trusting soul the faith is given
That this life's dreams shall prove the truths
   of heaven.

TRUTH

Thou long disowned, reviled, opprest,
  Strange friend of human kind,
Seeking through weary years a rest
  Within our heart to find.

How late thy bright and awful brow
  Breaks through these clouds of sin !
Hail, Truth Divine ! we know thee now,
  Angel of God, come in !

Come, though with purifying fire
  And desolating sword,
Thou of all nations the desire,
  Earth waits Thy cleansing word.

✠

Struck by the lightning of Thy glance
Let old oppressions die !
Before Thy cloudless countenance
Let fear and falsehood fly !

Anoint our eyes with healing grace
To see as ne'er before
Our Father, in our brother's face,
Our Master, in His poor.

Flood our dark life with golden day !
Convince, subdue, enthrall !
Then to a mightier yield Thy sway,
And Love be all in all !

Jan. 1860.

THE QUEST

"Whither shall I go from Thy spirit? or whither shall
I flee from Thy presence?"

I CANNOT find Thee! Still on restless pinion
My spirit beats the void where Thou dost
dwell ;
I wander lost through all Thy vast dominion,
And shrink beneath Thy light ineffable.

I cannot find Thee! E'en when most adoring
Before Thy throne, I bend in lowliest prayer ;
Beyond these bounds of thought, my thought
upsoaring
From farthest quest comes back ; Thou art
not there.

Yet high above the limits of my seeing,
　And folded far within the inmost heart,
And deep below the deeps of conscious being,
　Thy splendor shineth ; there, O God, Thou
　　art.

I cannot lose Thee ! Still in Thee abiding
　The end is clear, how wide soe'er I roam ;
The Hand that holds the worlds my steps is
　　guiding,
　And I must rest at last, in Thee, my home.

IN WAR TIME — 1863

WHY wilt thou ask, O doubting friend,
　　Where are the poets of these days?
Not yet is found a voice to blend
　　Our wail of woe, our psalm of praise.

Some laurel leaves of graceful rhyme
　　Wreathe here and there some victor's brow,
But the great poems for this time
　　Cannot be written — Oh not now!

Not now, while hand and heart and brain
　　For deeds of sternest toil are strung,
And precious life-blood drops like rain,
　　Can half our pride or grief be sung.

When the young Bayard of our race
Fell fighting with his dusky throng,
Close clasped for aye in death's embrace,
O friend! was this a time for song?

We weep and watch, we work and pray;
We hail the dawn that far exceeds
The noontide of our peaceful day;
But all our utterance is in deeds.

But wait till out of pain and strife
Our new and nobler peace is born;
Wait till the nation's coming life
Moves radiant through the gates of morn.

Then where the share was deepest driven
Shall glow the autumn's choicest store,
And where the billows swelled to heaven
Seek ocean's treasures on the shore.

Then look and listen ! then when Art
  To perfect shape shall freely grow,
And forms of grace instinctive start,
  The marble breathe, the canvas glow.

And then, in that accepted hour,
  On waves of mingling melody
Shall rise our song of praise and power,
  The choral anthem of the free !

TO G. S.

OF all the days that gild the gladsome year,
Not the first freshness of the vernal time,
Nor the refulgent pomp of summer's prime
Giveth to me such warm and heartfelt cheer
As the sweet season that brings in the morn
With roseate flush tempered with golden haze,
And fabled splendors of the Orient lays,
On glowing woods and fields of ripened corn;
How like a life by purest goodness filled;
Its wise deeds as the ripe and garnered fruit;
Its wild hopes chastened, and its tumults stilled

In air serene of thought entranced and mute.
O friend! this hand in flattery unskilled
For thee alone thus strikes this wandering
 lute.

Oct. 1866.

NO MORE SEA

LIFE of our life, and Light of all our seeing,
  How shall we rest on any hope but Thee?
What time our souls, to Thee for refuge fleeing,
  Long for the home where there is no more
  sea?

For still this sea of life, with endless wailing,
  Dashes above our heads its blinding spray,
And vanquished hearts, sick with remorse and
  failing,
  Moan like the waves at set of autumn day.

And ever round us swells the insatiate ocean
  Of sin and doubt that lures us to our grave;

When its wild billows with their mad commotion
  Would sweep us down — then only Thou
  canst save.

And deep and dark the fearful gloom unlighted,
  Of that untried and all-surrounding sea,
On whose bleak shore arriving lone, benighted,
  We fall and lose ourselves at last — in Thee.

Yea! in Thy life our little lives are ended,
  Into Thy depths our trembling spirits fall ;
In Thee enfolded, gathered, comprehended,
  As holds the sea her waves — Thou hold'st
  us all.

Aug. 1870.

TO L. M. C.

THE hastening year brings round once more,
    dear friend,
This welcome day which to the earth did lend
Such grace as sent you here awhile to live ;
Wherefore due thanks I ever duly give,
Knowing too well what stores of ripened thought,
What works of love, in shapely order wrought,
What inspiration waiting hearts to fill,
What bright designs, traced out with patient
    skill,
What converse sweet, what counsel wise and
    clear,
The world and I had missed, without you here.

Dear friend, be happy ! Be the lengthened way
Transfigured in the retrospect to-day !
Sunk out of sight, its vales of pain and grief,
Its radiant heights stand forth in clear relief,
And all the brightness of the past be thrown
Forward, to where Love waits to claim his own.

Feb. 1871.

WHOM BUT THEE

FROM past regret and present faithlessness,
From the deep shadow of foreseen distress,
And from the nameless weariness that grows
As life's long day seems wearing to its close ;

Thou Life within my life, than self more near !
Thou veilèd Presence infinitely clear !
From all illusive shows of sense I flee,
To find my centre and my rest in Thee.

Below all depths Thy saving mercy lies,
Through thickest glooms I see Thy light arise,
Above the highest heavens Thou art not found
More surely than within this earthly round.

Take part with me against these doubts that
    rise
And seek to throne Thee far in distant skies !
Take part with me against this self that dares
Assume the burden of these sins and cares !

How shall I call Thee who art always here,
How shall I praise Thee who art still most dear,
What may I give Thee save what Thou hast
    given,
And whom but Thee have I in earth or heaven ?

    Aug. 1871.

IN MEMORIAM F. D. B.

Dec. 4, 1871.

To pass through life beloved as few are loved,
To prove the joys of earth as few have proved,
And still to keep the soul's white robe unstained,
Such is the victory that thou hast gained.

How few, like thine, the pilgrim feet that come
Unworn, unwounded to the heavenly home!
Yet He who guides in sorrow's sorest need
As well by pleasant paths His own may lead.

And Love, that guards where wintry tempests
    beat,
To thee was shelter from the summer heat.
What need for grief to blight or cares annoy
The heart whose God was her exceeding joy ?

And so that radiant path, all sweet and pure,
Found fitting close in perfect peace secure ;
No haste to go, no anxious wish to stay,
No childish terror of the untried way.

But wrapped in trance of holy thought and
    prayer,
Yet full of human tenderness and care,
Undimmed its lustre and unchilled its love,
Thy spirit passed to cloudless light above.

In the far North, where over frosts and gloom
The midnight skies with rosy brightness bloom,

There comes in all the year one day complete,
Wherein the sunset and the sunrise meet.

So in the region of thy fearless faith,
No hour of darkness marked the approach of
 death,
But ere the evening splendor was withdrawn,
Fair flushed the light along the hills of dawn.

OUT OF THE SHADOW

"Rejoice ye, and be glad with her, all ye that love her: rejoice for joy with her, all ye that mourn for her."
— Is. lxvi. 10.

GENTLE friends who gather here,
Drop no unavailing tear,
With no gloom surround this bier.

Bid this weary frame opprest,
Welcome to its longed-for rest
On the fair earth's sheltering breast

And the spirit freed from clay,
Give glad leave to soar away,
Singing, to the eternal day.

When this sentient life began,
Love of nature, love of man
Through its kindling pulses ran ;

Eagerly these eyes looked forth
Questioning the teeming earth
For its stores of truth and worth.

Head and heart with schemes were rife,
Longing for some noble strife,
Planning for some perfect life ;

But the Father's love decreed
Other work and other meed,
And by ways unsought did lead ;

Turned aside the out-stretched hand,
Bade the feet inactive stand,
Checked the work that thought had planned ;

And on eyes that loved to gaze
Upon light's intensest rays
Dropped a veil of gentle haze.

How the musing spirit burned !
How the wilful nature yearned,
And its sacred limits spurned !

Known, O Father, unto Thee,
All the long captivity
Of the soul, at last set free ;

And how hard it was to see
Thy great harvests silently
Whitening upon land and lea ;

And to watch the reaper's throng,
Filling all the vales with song,
As they bore their sheaves along.

And to Thee, O pitying God,
Known Thy grace that overflowed
All that still and sacred road,

Where Thy patience brought relief
Following in Thy path of grief,
Thou of suffering souls the chief !

Yet, since Thou hast stooped to say,
" Cast that out-worn robe away,
Come and rest with me to-day, —

"Come to larger life and power,
Come to strength renewed each hour,
Come to truth's unfailing dower ; " —

To the dear ones gathered here
Make Thy loving purpose clear,
And Thy light shine round this bier.

1872.

LINES FOR MUSIC

As the lost who vainly wander,
　As the blind who widely roam,
Vexed with doubt, our spirits ponder
　Till we come to Thee, — our home.

As the mother fond watch keepeth,
　As the shepherd knows his sheep,
So Thine eye that never sleepeth
　All Thine own in sight doth keep.

As the wave is lost in ocean,
As the day-star melts in light,
Draw to Thee each wavering motion,
Thou whose coming ends our night.

Feb. 1873.

VESPER HYMN

THE day is done ; the weary day of thought
    and toil is past,
Soft falls the twilight cool and gray, on the tired
    earth at last :
By wisest teachers wearied, by gentlest friends
    opprest,
In Thee alone, the soul, out-worn, refreshment
    finds and rest.

Bend, gracious Spirit, from above, like these
    o'erarching skies,
And to Thy firmament of love lift up these
    longing eyes ;

And folded by Thy sheltering Hand, in refuge
    still and deep,
Let blessed thoughts from Thee descend, as
    drop the dews of sleep.

And when refreshed, the soul once more puts
    on new life and power ;
Oh let Thine image, Lord, alone, gild the first
    waking hours.
Let that dear Presence rise and glow, fairer
    than morn's first ray,
And Thy pure radiance overflow the splendor
    of the day.

So in the hastening evening, so in the coming
    morn,
When deeper slumber shall be given, and fresher
    life be born,

Shine out, true Light ! to guide my way amid
 that deepening gloom,
And rise, O Morning Star, the first that day-
 spring to illume.

I cannot dread the darkness, where Thou wilt
 watch o'er me,
Nor smile to greet the sunrise, unless Thy smile
 I see ;
Creator, Saviour, Comforter ! on Thee my soul
 is cast ;
At morn, at night, in earth, in heaven, be Thou
 my First and Last.

Oct. 1874.

COLLECT — ASCENSION DAY

Grant, we beseech thee, Almighty God, that like as we do believe thy only begotten Son our Lord Jesus Christ to have ascended into the heavens; so we may also in heart and mind thither ascend, and with him continually dwell, who liveth and reigneth with thee and the Holy Ghost, one God, world without end.

Thou hast gone up again,
Thou, who didst first come down,
Thou hast gone up to reign,
Gone up, from Cross to Crown.

Beyond the opening sky
No more Thy face we see ;
Yet draw our souls on high,
That we may dwell with Thee.

Up to those regions blest,
Where faith has fullest sway,
Up to Thine endless rest,
Up to Thy cloudless day,

Up to that glowing life,
Up to that perfect peace,
Unvexed by doubt or strife,
Where care and conflict cease,

Up, up to where Thou art,
Fount of unwasting Love,
Up to that mighty Heart,
All its great power to prove.

Not now for distant heaven
Or future life we pray,
    Lord, let Thy grace be given
To make us Thine to-day.

Here, hold us in Thy hand,
Here, by Thy spirit guide,
    So shall our hearts ascend,
And still with Thee abide.

May 14, 1874.

COLLECT FOR SECOND SUNDAY
AFTER EPIPHANY

Almighty and everlasting God, who dost govern all things in heaven and earth ; mercifully hear the supplications of thy people, and grant us thy peace all the days of our life; through Jesus Christ our Lord.

GRANT us Thy peace, down from Thy presence
    falling
As on the thirsty earth cool night-dews sweet,
Grant us Thy peace, to Thy pure paths recall-
    ing,
    From devious ways, our worn and wandering
    feet.

Grant us Thy peace, through winning and
    through losing,
  Through gloom and gladness of our pilgrim
    way,
Grant us Thy peace, safe in Thy love's
    enclosing,
  Thou, who all things in heaven and earth
    dost sway.

Give us Thy peace, not as the world has given
  In momentary rays that fitful gleamed,
But calm, deep, sure, the peace of spirits shriven
  Of hearts surrendered and of souls redeemed.

Grant us Thy peace, that like a deepening river
  Swells ever outward to a sea of praise.
O Thou, of peace the only Lord and Giver,
  Grant us Thy peace, O Saviour, all our days !

THANKSGIVING

" We bless Thee . . . for the means of grace and for the hope of glory."

FOR the rapt stillness of the place
Where sacred song and ordered prayer
Wait the unveiling of Thy face,
And seek Thy angels' joys to share ;

For souls won o'er to truth and right,
For wisdom dropping as the dew,
For Thy great WORD in lines of light,
Made visible to mortal view ;

For gladness of the summer morning,
For fair faint twilight's lingering ray,
For forest's and for field's adorning,
And the wild ocean's ceaseless play;

For flowers unsought, in desert places
Flashing enchantment on the sight;
For radiance on familiar faces
As they passed upward into light;

For blessings of the fruitful season,
For work and rest, for friends and home,
For the great gifts of thought and reason, —
To praise and bless Thee, Lord, we come.

Yes, and for weeping and for wailing,
For bitter hail and blighting frost,
For high hopes on the low earth trailing,
For sweet joys missed, for pure aims crost;

For lonely toil and tribulation,
And e'en for hidings of Thy face, —
For these Thy heralds of salvation,
Thy means and messengers of grace.

With joy supreme, with faith unbroken,
With worship passing thought or speech,
Of Thy dear love we hail each token,
And give Thee humble thanks for each.

For o'er our struggling and our sighing,
Now quenched in mist, now glimmering far
Above our living and our dying,
Hangs high in Heaven one beckoning star.

And when we gather up the story
Of all Thy mercies flowing free,
Crown of them all, that hope of glory,
Of growing ever nearer Thee.

www.ingramcontent.com/pod-product-compliance
Lightning Source LLC
Chambersburg PA
CBHW021639270326
41931CB00008B/1082